AF228626

BASEBALL

A&D Xtreme
BOLD HI-LO NONFICTION

An imprint of Abdo Publishing
abdobooks.com

BRENDAN FLYNN

TAKE IT TO THE XTREME!

GET READY FOR AN EXTREME ADVENTURE!
THE PAGES OF THIS BOOK WILL TAKE YOU INTO
THE THRILLING WORLD OF BASEBALL.
WHEN YOU HAVE FINISHED READING THIS BOOK, TAKE THE
XTREME CHALLENGE ON PAGE 45 ABOUT WHAT YOU'VE LEARNED!

ABDOBOOKS.COM

102022
012023

Design: Series Designer Kelly Doudna, Mighty Media, Inc.
Production: Mighty Media, Inc.
Editor: Liz Salzmann
Cover Photograph: Frank Jansky/AP Images
Interior Photographs: AL BEHRMAN/AP Images, pp. 34–35; Alan Tan
    Photography/Shutterstock Images, pp. 4–5; Alex Brandon/AP Images,
    pp. 38–39; AP Images, pp. 10–11, 16–17, 28–29; Carolyn Franks/Shutterstock
    Images, p. 1; David Lee/Shutterstock Images, p. 44; Doug Sheridan/AP
    Images, pp. 18–19; JASON LEE/AP Images, pp. 24–25; John Lent/AP Images,
    pp. 14–15; Keith J Finks/Shutterstock Images, pp. 30–31; Library of Congress,
    pp. 8–9, 32–33; Mark Goldman/AP Images, pp. 36–37; PAT SULLIVAN/AP
    Images, pp. 22–23; Picasa/Wikimedia Commons, pp. 40–41, 42–43; RAS/
    AP Images, pp. 20–21; TOM SANDE/AP Images, pp. 26–27; Wikimedia
    Commons, pp. 6–7, 12–13, 13 (inset)
Design Elements: ayagiz/iStockphoto (hexagon texture); huseyintuncer/
    iStockphoto (turf); LeArchitecto/iStockphoto (lights); Roman Bykhalets/
    iStockphoto (dots)

LIBRARY OF CONGRESS CONTROL NUMBER: 2022940525

PUBLISHER'S CATALOGING-IN-PUBLICATION DATA
Names: Flynn, Brendan, author.
Title: Baseball / by Brendan Flynn
Description: Minneapolis, Minnesota : Abdo Publishing, 2023 | Series: Xtreme
    moments in sports | Includes online resources and index.
Identifiers: ISBN 9781532199271 (lib. bdg.) | ISBN 9781098274474 (ebook)
Subjects: LCSH: Baseball--Juvenile literature. | Field sports--Juvenile literature. |
    Baseball--History--Juvenile literature. | Sports--History--Juvenile literature.
Classification: DDC 796.357--dc23

TABLE OF CONTENTS

BASEBALL BEGINNINGS 4

BABE CALLS HIS SHOT 6

ROBINSON'S DEBUT....................................10

THE RYAN EXPRESS 18

IRON MAN 24

REVERSE THE CURSE 30

STRIKEOUT MACHINE 36

CUBS WIN!...40

THE FUTURE OF BASEBALL 44

XTREME CHALLENGE................................45

GLOSSARY..46

ONLINE RESOURCES 47

INDEX 48

CHAPTER 1

BASEBALL BEGINNINGS

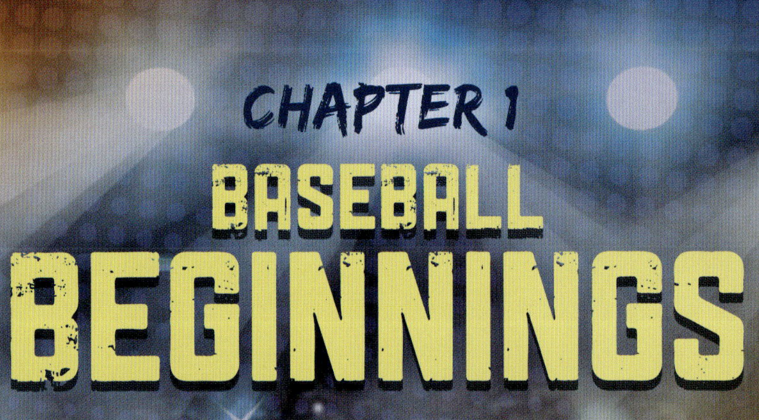

Baseball dates back to the 1800s. The **National League** was founded in 1876. The **American League** came along in 1901. Together, these leagues form Major League Baseball (MLB). Over the years, there have been many amazing baseball games and players.

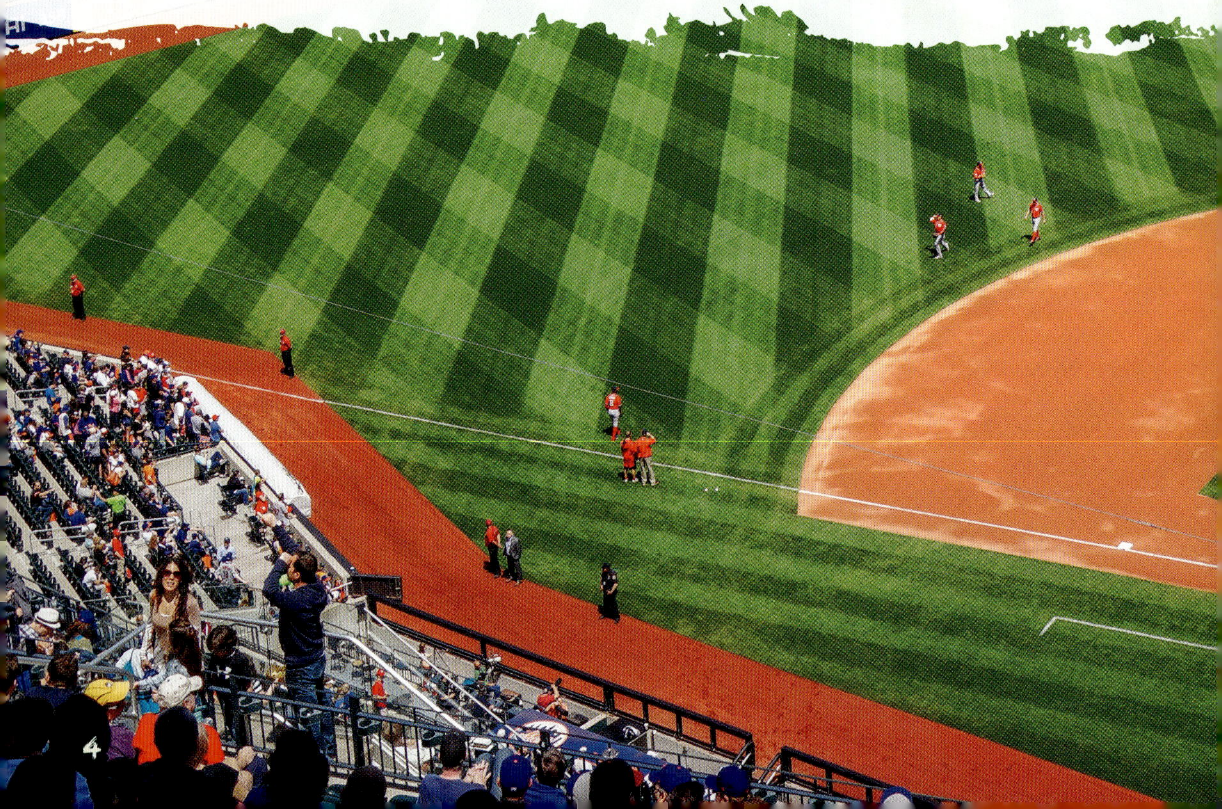

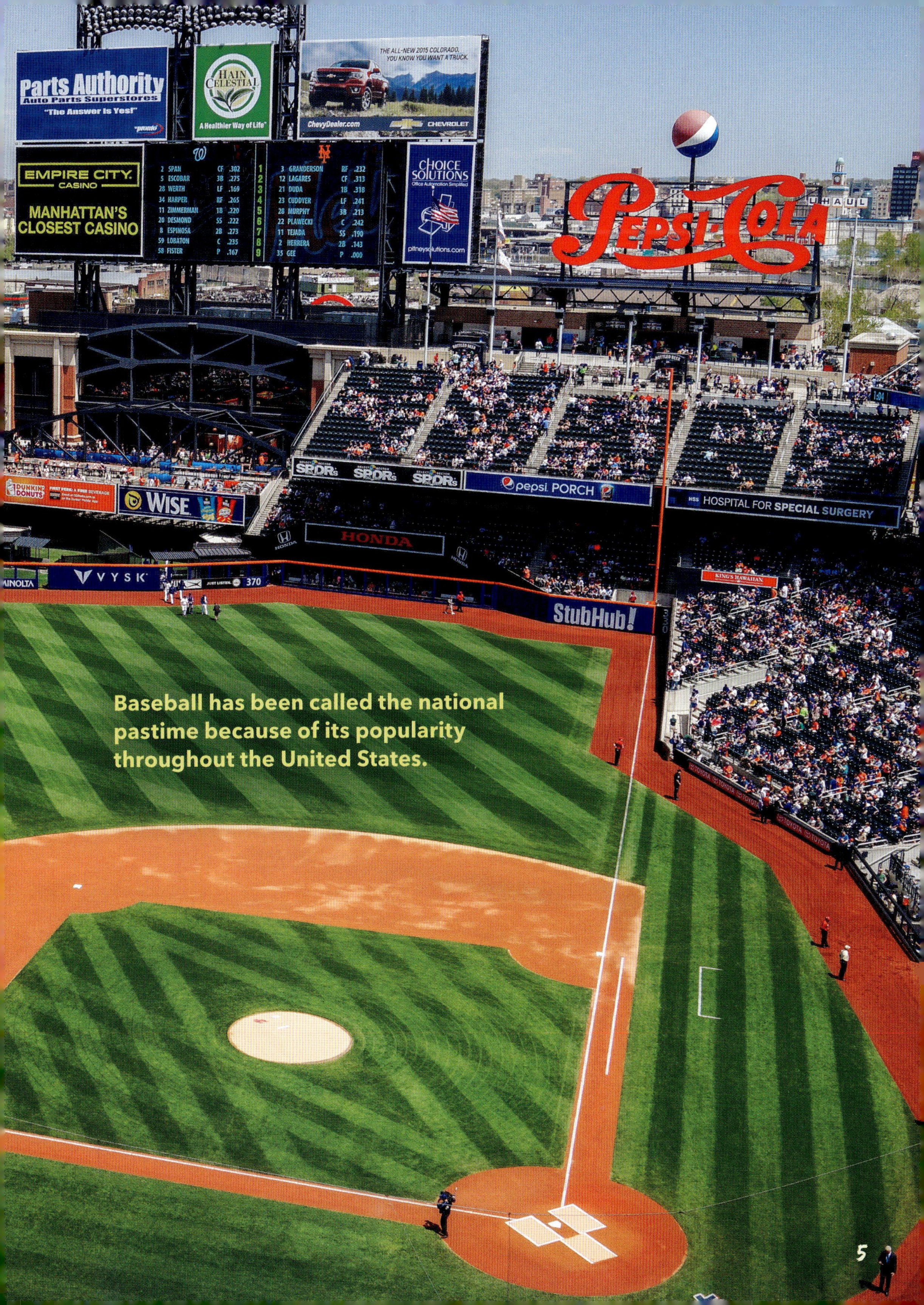

Baseball has been called the national pastime because of its popularity throughout the United States.

CHAPTER 2

BABE
CALLS HIS SHOT

It was Game 3 of the 1932 World **Series**. The New York Yankees had won the first two games against the Chicago Cubs. Game 3 was tied 4–4. Babe Ruth stepped up to bat for the Yankees. The Cubs players and fans shouted and booed. They were trying to **distract** him.

Ruth started his career as a
pitcher with the Boston Red Sox.

Ruth was not bothered. He calmly stepped out of the batter's box. He looked at the Cubs **bench** and pointed at the center-field fence with his bat. Then he slammed the next pitch over the wall where he had pointed. Ruth's famous "called shot" put the Yankees ahead. They went on to **sweep** the Cubs to win the World **Series**.

XTREME FACT

Babe Ruth was a power hitter like few others in history. In many seasons he hit more home runs by himself than some entire teams!

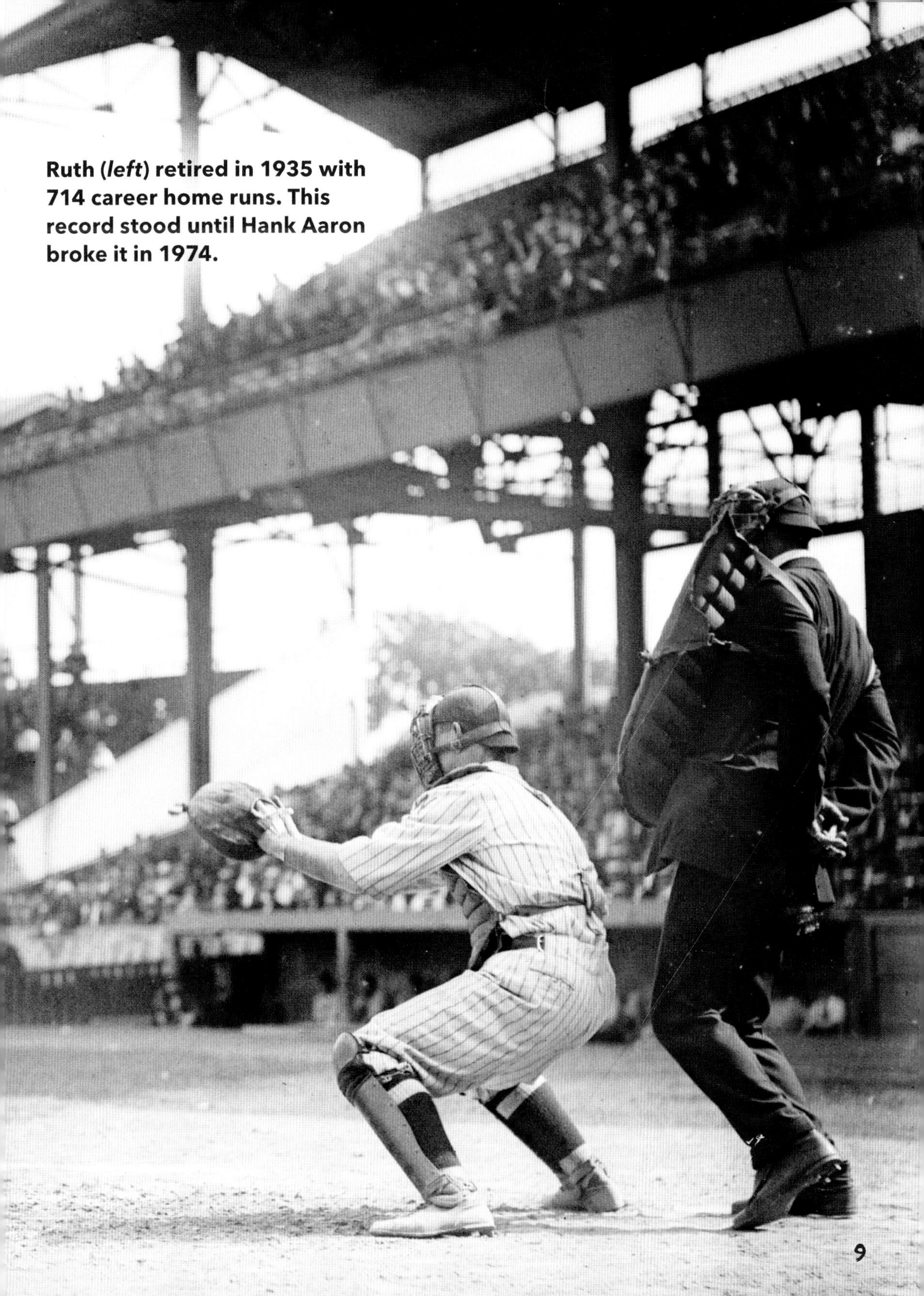

Ruth (*left*) retired in 1935 with 714 career home runs. This record stood until Hank Aaron broke it in 1974.

CHAPTER 3

ROBINSON'S DEBUT

April 15, 1947, was Opening Day at Ebbets Field in Brooklyn, New York. The hometown Dodgers faced the Boston Braves. Some fans could not believe their eyes. A Black man named Jackie Robinson was playing first base for the Dodgers.

Robinson played first base during his first season with the Dodgers. After that, he played second base for the rest of his career.

For a long time, parts of the United States were **segregated** by race. Baseball followed those rules too. The Negro Leagues offered a way for the best Black ballplayers to show their talents. But these players were not allowed to join MLB teams.

In 1945, Robinson played for the Kansas City Monarchs in the Negro League.

Some MLB leaders believed **segregation** was wrong. One of these people was Brooklyn Dodgers general manager Branch Rickey. Rickey took the first step toward ending segregation in baseball. In October 1945, he signed Jackie Robinson to play for the Dodgers. Robinson spent the 1946 season with the Montreal Royals, a Dodgers **minor league** team.

Robinson (*right*) scores after hitting a home run in a Montreal Royals game against the Jersey City Giants.

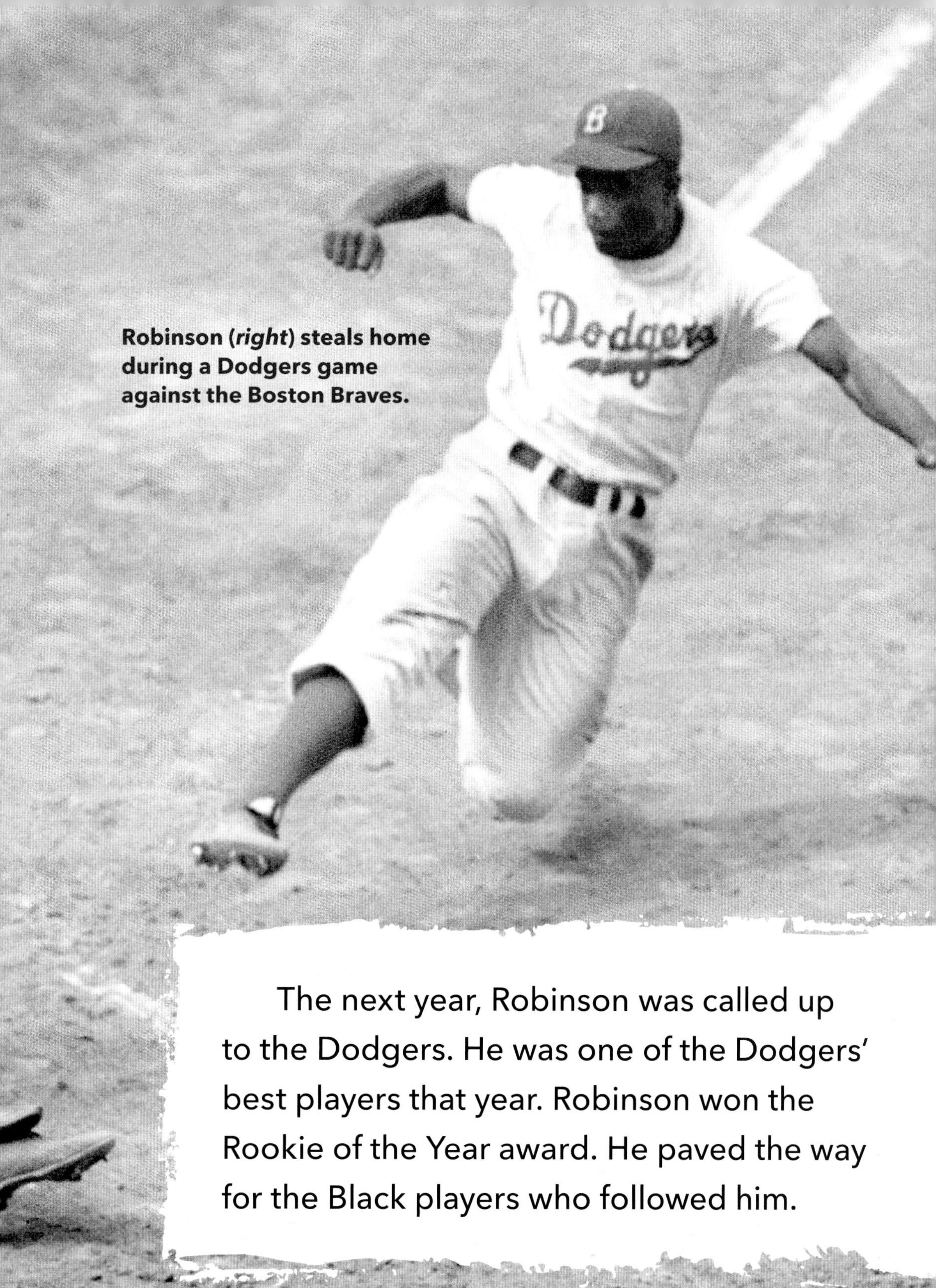

Robinson (*right*) steals home during a Dodgers game against the Boston Braves.

The next year, Robinson was called up to the Dodgers. He was one of the Dodgers' best players that year. Robinson won the Rookie of the Year award. He paved the way for the Black players who followed him.

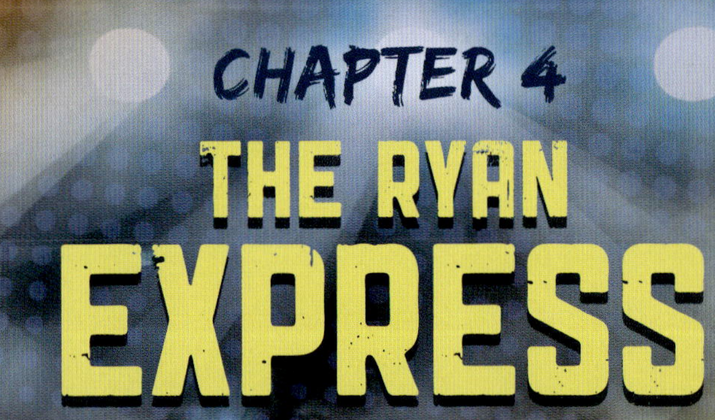

Ryan played for four MLB teams. He finished his career with the Texas Rangers.

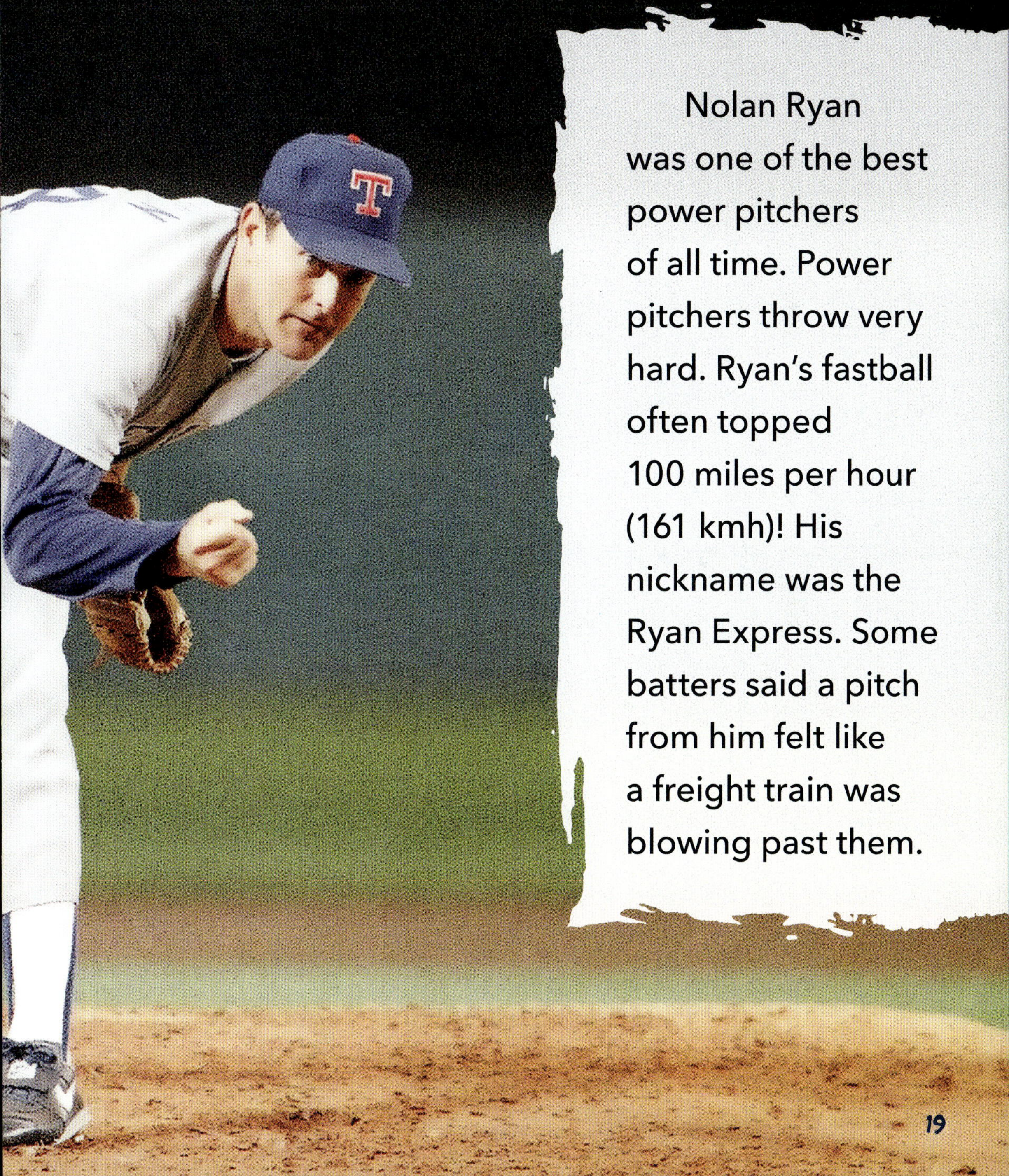

Nolan Ryan
was one of the best
power pitchers
of all time. Power
pitchers throw very
hard. Ryan's fastball
often topped
100 miles per hour
(161 kmh)! His
nickname was the
Ryan Express. Some
batters said a pitch
from him felt like
a freight train was
blowing past them.

Ryan (*second from left*) was playing for the California Angels when he pitched his first four no-hitters.

Ryan struck out more batters than any pitcher in MLB history. Some days, nobody could get a hit against him. When a team goes an entire game without getting a hit, it's called a no-hitter. Ryan threw seven no-hitters. This is three more than any other pitcher.

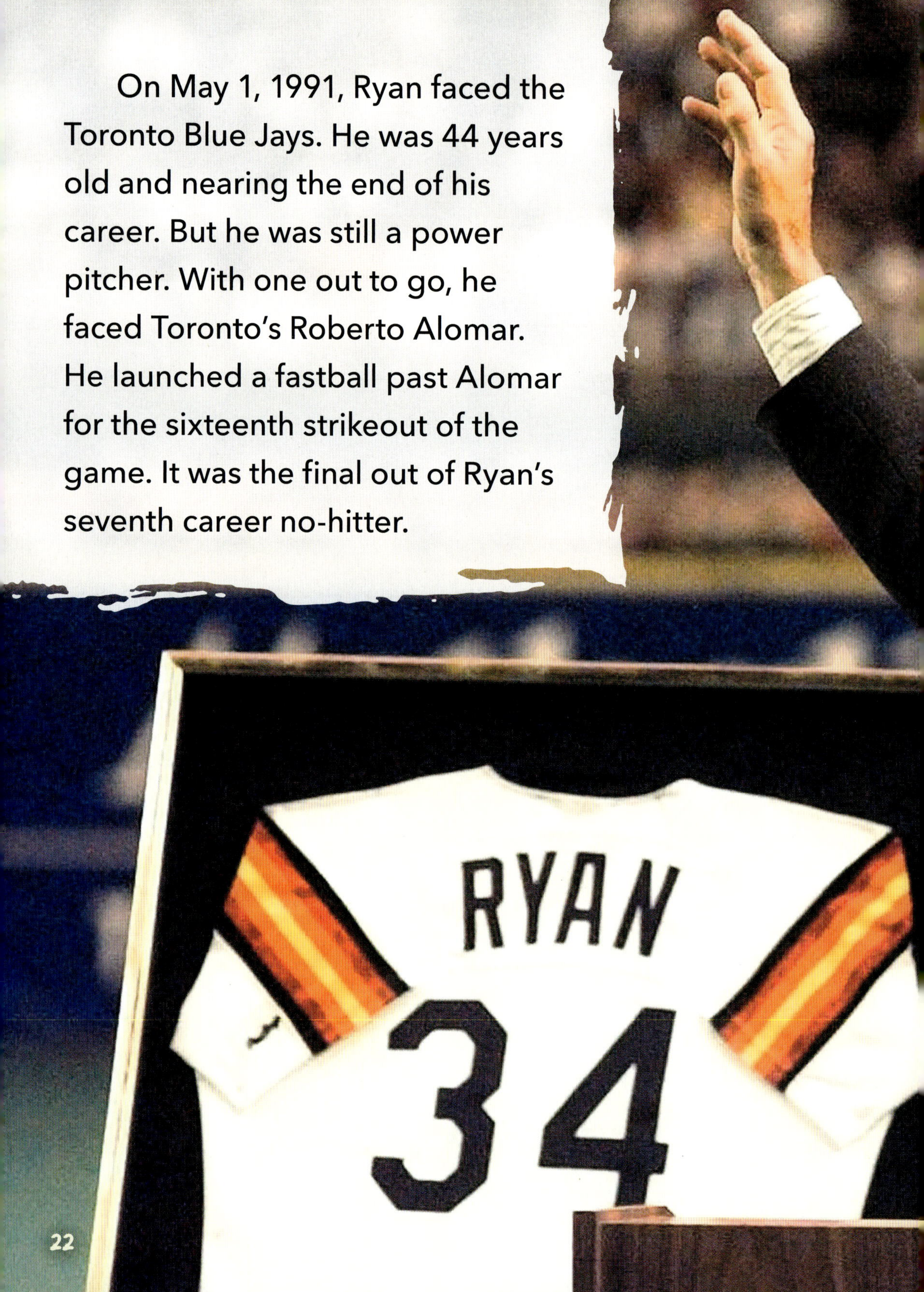

On May 1, 1991, Ryan faced the Toronto Blue Jays. He was 44 years old and nearing the end of his career. But he was still a power pitcher. With one out to go, he faced Toronto's Roberto Alomar. He launched a fastball past Alomar for the sixteenth strikeout of the game. It was the final out of Ryan's seventh career no-hitter.

Ryan retired in 1993 after 27 years as an MLB player. His number was later retired by three of the teams he played for, including the Houston Astros.

CHAPTER 5

IRON MAN

Cal Ripken Jr. joined the Baltimore Orioles in 1981. He soon became one of the best players in the league. He was also one of the most dependable. Starting May 30, 1982, Ripken played in every game the rest of the year. The streak lasted through the next year. And the next.

Ripken (*left*) was known as an excellent shortstop. He won two Gold Gloves during his career.

By 1995, Ripken still hadn't missed a single game. He was nearing one of MLB's most amazing records. Lou Gehrig had played in 2,130 straight games from 1925 to 1939. Most thought Gehrig's record would never be broken. But on September 6, 1995, Ripken made it to 2,131 games.

**Gehrig played for the
New York Yankees
from 1923 to 1939.**

The Orioles played the California Angels at home that night. And of course, Ripken was in the **lineup**. The Baltimore fans gave him a **standing ovation**. Ripken jogged a lap around the stadium. He shook hands and high-fived fans. He thanked them for their support. Cal Ripken Jr. had become MLB's new Iron Man.

XTREME FACT

Ripken continued to play every game for three more years. When he finally sat out, his streak had reached 2,632 games.

CHAPTER 6

REVERSE THE CURSE

The Boston Red Sox is one of MLB's oldest teams. They won the first World **Series** in 1903. By 1918, they had won it four more times. But after the 1919 season, the team's owner needed money. So, he sold his best player, Babe Ruth, to the New York Yankees.

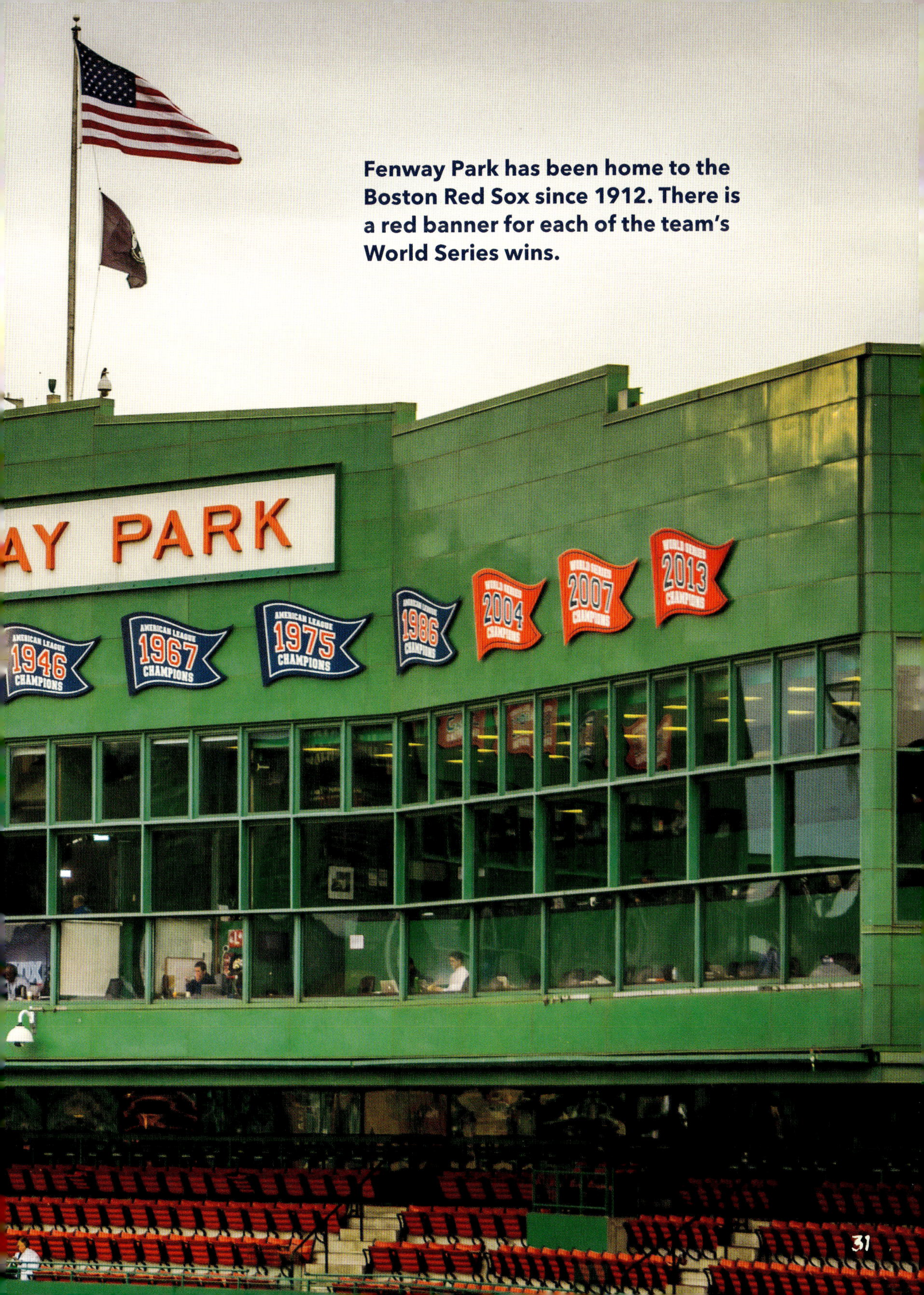

Fenway Park has been home to the Boston Red Sox since 1912. There is a red banner for each of the team's World Series wins.

Soon, the Yankees were the best team in baseball. The Red Sox fell apart. They made it to the World **Series** only four times in the next 86 years. And they lost each time. Many Boston fans believed that sending Ruth to the Yankees had put a curse on the Red Sox.

Ruth's (*second from right*) nickname was the Bambino. So people said the Red Sox losses were due to the "Curse of the Bambino."

Red Sox players celebrate their 2004 World Series win.

In 2004, the Red Sox and Yankees met in the playoffs. The Yankees won the first three games. They just needed one more win to end Boston's season. But the Red Sox rallied. They won four straight games to win the **series**. Then the Red Sox beat the St. Louis Cardinals in the World Series. The curse had been defeated!

CHAPTER 7

STRIKEOUT MACHINE

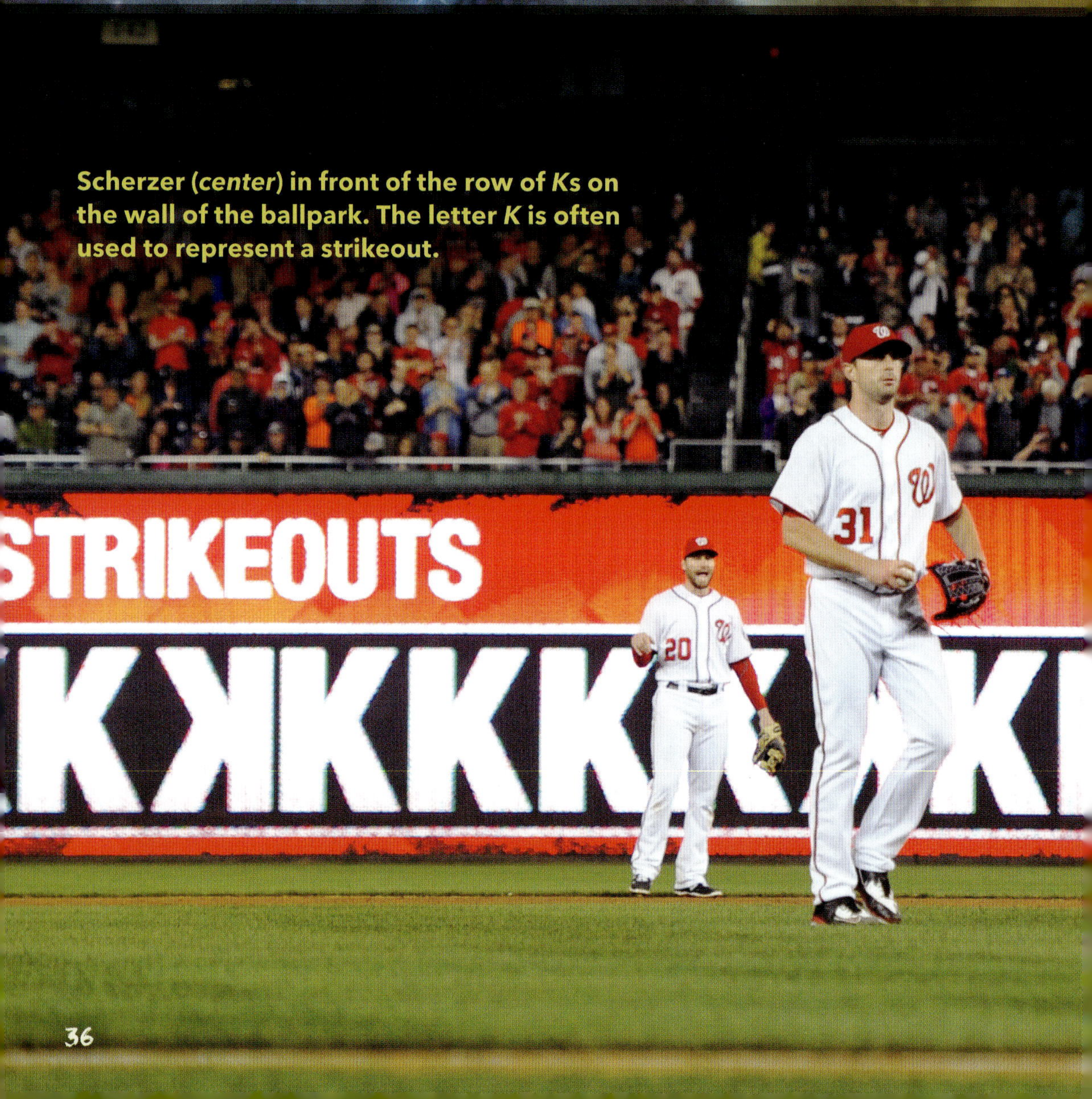

Scherzer (*center*) in front of the row of *K*s on the wall of the ballpark. The letter *K* is often used to represent a strikeout.

On May 11, 2016, the Washington Nationals played the Detroit Tigers. Nationals pitcher Max Scherzer was having a terrific game. With three outs to go, he'd struck out 18 Tigers batters. The MLB record for strikeouts in a nine-inning game is 20. Could Scherzer get three more?

XTREME FACT
Only three other
pitchers have struck
out 20 batters in
nine innings. They
are Randy Johnson,
Kerry Wood, and
Roger Clemens. And
Clemens did it twice!

In the ninth inning, Scherzer threw a fastball past Miguel Cabrera for strike three. Then Justin Upton swung and missed at a wicked slider for another strikeout. Scherzer had 20 strikeouts! Everyone was cheering for Scherzer to get one more. But James McCann grounded out to end the game. It wasn't a strikeout. But Scherzer had tied the record!

After the game, a teammate dumps water on Scherzer to celebrate his 20 strikeouts.

CHAPTER 8

CUBS WIN!

It was the tenth inning of Game 7 of the 2016 World **Series**. The Chicago Cubs led 8–7. They needed one more out to beat Cleveland. The batter hit a slow roller past the mound. Third baseman Kris Bryant charged in. He scooped up the ball and fired to first base. Anthony Rizzo caught it for the final out. Cubs win!

Cubs outfielder Ben Zobrist was named World Series MVP. He had ten hits in the series, including a double that scored the winning run in the final game.

The Cubs had been called baseball's lovable losers for a long time. They hadn't won a World **Series** since 1908. Chicago fans loved their Cubbies. They enjoyed sunny days watching ball games at Wrigley Field. They had fun whether their team won or lost. But winning a World Series was the most fun of all.

CHAPTER 9

THE FUTURE
OF BASEBALL

Baseball is still one of the biggest sports in the world. Every year, exciting new players become fan favorites. Keep watching to see what superstar players such as Mike Trout, Shohei Ohtani, Juan Soto, and Ronald Acuña do next.

CHALLENGE

TAKE THE QUIZ BELOW AND
PUT WHAT YOU'VE LEARNED TO THE TEST!

1) Why were fans surprised to see Jackie Robinson playing for the Dodgers in 1947?

2) How many career no-hitters did Nolan Ryan throw?

3) Who held the consecutive games record before Cal Ripken Jr. broke it?

4) What does the "Curse of the Bambino" mean?

5) What letter represents a strikeout?

GLOSSARY

American League—one of the two divisions in Major League Baseball.

bench—in baseball, a team's players who are not currently in the game.

debut—a first appearance.

distract—to cause someone to lose concentration or focus.

lineup—in baseball, the list of players in a game and the order in which they bat.

minor league—part of the four classes of professional baseball that are lower level than the major leagues.

National League—one of the two divisions in Major League Baseball.

segregate—to separate an individual or a group from a larger group, especially by race. An act or system of segregating is segregation.

series—a group of several games played by the same two teams. Whichever team wins most of the games wins the series.

standing ovation–when the people attending a play, sporting event, or other performance stand up and applaud to show enthusiastic approval or appreciation.

sweep–to win all the games in a series.

ONLINE RESOURCES

To learn more about baseball, please visit **abdobooklinks.com** or scan this QR code. These links are routinely monitored and updated to provide the most current information available.

INDEX

A

Acuña, Ronald, 44
Alomar, Roberto, 22
American League, 4, 11

B

Baltimore Orioles, 24, 28
Baseball Hall of Fame, 11
Boston Braves, 10
Boston Red Sox, 30, 32, 35
Brooklyn Dodgers, 10, 14, 17
Bryant, Kris, 41

C

Cabrera, Miguel, 39
California Angels, 28
Chicago Cubs, 6, 8, 41, 43
Clemens, Roger, 38

D

Detroit Tigers, 37
Doby, Larry, 11

E

Ebbets Field, 10

G

Gehrig, Lou, 26

H

home runs, 8, 34

J

Johnson, Randy, 38

K

Koufax, Sandy, 23

L

Los Angeles Angels, 34
Los Angeles Dodgers, 23

M

McCann, James, 39
minor league, 14
MLB, 4, 12, 14, 21, 26, 28, 30, 37,
Montreal Royals, 14

N

National League, 4
Negro Leagues, 12
New York Yankees, 6, 8, 30, 32, 35

O

Ohtani, Shohei, 34, 44

P

playoffs, 35

R

Rickey, Branch, 14
Ripken, Cal, Jr., 24, 26, 28, 29
Rizzo, Anthony, 41
Robinson, Jackie, 10, 11, 14, 17
Rookie of the Year, 17
Ruth, Babe, 6, 8, 30, 32, 34
Ryan, Nolan, 19, 21, 22, 23

S

Scherzer, Max, 37, 39
segregation, 12, 14
Soto, Juan, 44
St. Louis Cardinals, 35

T

Toronto Blue Jays, 22
Trout, Mike, 44

U

Upton, Justin, 39

W

Washington Nationals, 37
Wood, Kerry, 38
World Series, 6, 8, 30, 32, 35, 41, 43
Wrigley Field, 43